C FERRET

by Dennis Kelsey-Wood

© 2004 Dalmatian Press, LLC
All rights reserved. Printed in the U.S.A.

The DALMATIAN PRESS name and logo are trademarks
of Dalmatian Press, LLC, Franklin, Tennessee 37067.
No part of this book may be reproduced or copied in any form
without the written permission of Dalmatian Press, LLC.
Photos © Keith Allison
Editor *Mary Ginder*
Designer *Dan Waters*
ISBN: 1-40370-888-6

13472 Caring For Your Ferret
04 05 06 07 08 WWP 10 9 8 7 6 5 4 3 2 1

Ferrets: Biological Data

ADULT WEIGHT: 14 ounces to 4 pounds (400g to 2kg)

AVERAGE SIZE (ADULT): 14 to 24 inches (35 to 62cm)

LIFESPAN: 6–10 years (in captivity)

SEXUAL MATURITY: At six to eight months of age

BREEDING SEASON: March to September

ESTRUS CYCLE: Induced ovulator (eggs are shed by the act of mating).

GESTATION PERIOD: 40–44 days

LITTER SIZE: Six to nine kits, sometimes more

DEVELOPMENT: The kits are born blind, deaf, and naked. Fur is evident within 5–7 days. Eyes and ears open at 22–35 days.

WEANING: At six to nine weeks

Acknowledgments

Special thanks to Peter Pearson and the Wakefield Ferret and Small Animal Rescue.

Contents

INTRODUCING THE FERRET: Is It the Right Pet for You?

Although ferrets have been domesticated for many centuries, the average person knows surprisingly little about them—half-truths and legends are more common than facts. More often than not, the ferret has been unfairly and even harshly characterized. In the following chapters, you'll get to know the true facts about this fascinating and delightful animal so that you can decide whether a ferret would be a suitable pet for you and your family.

What Is a Ferret?

The ferret is a carnivorous (meat-eating) mammal which is part of the biological family *Mustelidae*, also known as the mustelids.

The pet ferret is a domesticated polecat.

This group contains ferrets as well as weasels, minks, polecats, martens, badgers, skunks, wolverines, and other less well-known "weasel-like" animals.

The pet ferret is a domesticated polecat, generally thought to be descended from the European polecat, whose scientific name is *Mustela putorius*. The domestic ferret has the name *Mustela putorius furo* to distinguish it from its wild ancestor. *Mustela* is Latin for weasel, while *putorius* derives from the Latin word *putor*, meaning a bad smell (later we will discuss this matter of odor and the reasons why it has become unjustly associated with ferrets). *Furo* is the Latin word for "thief," which has come via Old French as *furet*, and *fyrette* or *firette* in Middle English, to become the word "ferret" we use today.

There are just three species of polecats: the European, already mentioned; the Turkestan (*Mustela eversmanni*), native to northern Asia and China, though it has now spread into Western Europe; and the Black-footed ferret (*Mustela nigripes*) of North America, which is an endangered species. The nearest relatives to the ferret, other than those already cited, are raccoons, coatimundis, pandas, bears, viverrids (civets, genets and mongooses), hyenas, dogs and cats—placed in the likely order of distance as relatives. Ferrets are not related to rats, mice, squirrels, or other rodents.

Natural History

Wild ferrets (polecats) are found in a wide variety of habitats, from lowland forests to meadows and semi-deserts. They may also take up residence in agricultural regions, living in outbuildings—even old houses—where they capitalize on the easy availability of small rodents. The Turkestan polecat is generally active by day, while its European relative is more crepuscular (active at dawn and dusk) or nocturnal. However, these animals are able to adjust their periods of activity quite easily, and, if they are subject to human or other persecution, will tend to become more active at times that seem safer, night instead of day, or vice versa.

Ferrets either dig their own den for sleeping or take over an unused burrow dug by a rabbit, fox, or other animal. They may

Wild ferrets live in a variety of habitats ranging from lowland forest to semi-desert.

spend a great many hours sleeping, depending on how good the local food supply is. In places where food is hard to find, they must devote more time to traveling. Wild ferrets are loners by nature, coming together mainly for breeding purposes.

Ferrets in the wild hunt and eat small mammals and rodents such as rats, mice, hamsters, gerbils, voles, ground squirrels, and rabbits. They will also take reptiles, lizards, amphibians, bird eggs, baby birds, and any other birds that come within their reach. Ferrets eat some invertebrates (worms and insects), but typically do not eat fish. Fruits and vegetables play little role in their diet since ferrets are unable to digest

DON'T BELIEVE WHAT YOU HEAR.
People may tell you that the ferret, like the mongoose, is immune to snake bites. It's not true for the ferret (nor is it true for the mongoose). The ferret is simply very good at attacking a snake so quickly that he delivers a fatal bite to the snake's neck before the snake can bite *him*.

their tough cellulose walls; however, wild ferrets do obtain
some fruits and vegetables via the partially digested contents of
their prey's stomachs.

Enemies of ferrets include wolves, jackals, foxes, wild cats,
feral dogs, large snakes, and birds of prey. However, humans
are their biggest enemy, either directly or indirectly.
Development often destroys their natural habitats or the
species (such as prairie dogs) upon which the ferrets prey.

The ferret typically lives for six to ten years in captivity, but
less than that in the wild. However, domestic ferrets have been
known to attain 15 years and a well-cared-for pet can easily
reach 10 to 12 years.

A male ferret is called a "hob," a female is a "jill," and a youngster is a "kit." With respect to size, a hob may grow as long as
24 inches (62 cms) while a jill will be much smaller, as little as
14 inches (35 cms). The ferret's tail accounts for nearly half of
its length.

Adult weight is 2–4 lbs for males and 1–3 pounds for females.
Ferrets gain weight as winter approaches—as much as 20 to 40
percent of their body weight—and then lose that weight in the
spring. They also grow thicker coats in the winter and then
molt (shed) in the spring.

Domestic History

Some people believe that the ferret was first domesticated by the
ancient Egyptians—perhaps even predating the cat. However,
the evidence is debatable. Artifacts and paintings of weasel-
like animals are hardly accurate for identification purposes.

It is possible that depictions credited as being ferrets are in fact the Ichneumon (*Herpestes ichneumon*), also commonly known as Pharaoh's rat or the Egyptian mongoose.

It is more likely that domestication began in the Roman period, possibly about 300 B.C. There is evidence that the Romans and Greeks used ferrets to help reduce rabbit populations on some Balearic and Aegean islands.

Possibly the Romans (and certainly the Normans after 1066) took a semi-domesticated form of the ferret to Britain. There, as in other European countries, it was a well-established domestic animal by the Middle Ages—domesticated primarily reason of hunting rabbits rather than as a household companion pet as we think of them today. The sport of "ferreting"—using ferrets to flush rabbits out of their burrows—dates back at least to the Norman period in English history (approx. 1000–1500 A.D.). Ferrets were often used on ships to keep rodents under control and may have been brought to America as early as the 1600s.

What You Need to Know About Ferrets Before You Buy One

Many pet owners do not consider their decision to take on a pet as carefully as they should. Each year millions of pets are subjected to neglect, abuse, and abandonment because owners do not appreciate and honor the commitment they made.

Ferrets are playful, inquisitive creatures which make delightful pets—provided that you understand their unique qualities (they are not like dogs and cats!) and can accept them for what they are. In particular, prospective ferret owners need to be aware of and accept the ferret's natural musky odor and its instinctive tendency to nip, whether playfully or as a way of protecting itself.

ODORS
Like the other members of the Mustelid family, ferrets have anal scent glands which they use to emit a musky odor in order to deter predators (this is sometimes called "poofing.")

A member of the Mustelid family, the ferret ejects a musky-smelling odor from its anal glands when it is frightened or threatened.

Even a domesti-cated ferret will display its natural predatory instincts.

Ferrets also have musk glands around their face and on their body. Their natural, everyday odor has more to do with these musk glands (and hormones) than with the anal scent glands. To put this into perspective: all animals have a natural body odor and many also have scent glands, including cats and dogs, especially males. These are used when the animal is in a fearful state or when marking territory—or both, depending on the species. Urine and fecal matter also create odor.

Before you buy or adopt a ferret, you need to know whether their natural scent is tolerable for you. Only by experience of this—at a friend or breeder's home—can you really know if this would be acceptable. Nearly all ferrets are neutered at an early age and this greatly reduces their odor. **As with any type of pet, thorough cleaning greatly minimizes odor problems. Ignore this and a home will slowly build up ferret odors.** For more on odor control, see Chapter 4.

BITING
From an early age, ferrets love to play. Nipping and hanging on with their teeth are instinctive to them: that is how they obtain food in the wild. In captivity, however, they must be trained to minimize this behavior when handled. **The most important thing you can do to avoid problems with biting and aggression is to make sure that the ferret you purchase cooperates when handled.** If the animal is aggressive when you first hold it, that is not likely to change when you get it home.

A playful nip from a youngster is rarely painful, but from an adult ferret it can really hurt—just as it would if you were

Obviously, nipping needs to be subdued when ferrets are interacting with their human companions.

bitten by a dog, a cat, or even a hamster. Ferrets that are handled and trained correctly, however, will not display aggressive biting tendencies. If they do, it will be for one of the following reasons: they have been handled incorrectly or not frequently enough; they were allowed to get away with biting as youngsters; they have an inherently aggressive nature due to poor breeding; or they may have an injury or internal disorder that creates pain even when they are handled gently.

Ferrets are individuals and each has its own personality. Some are very gentle, others more robust in their play. Males are normally larger, so will be more powerful, but are not any more likely to be aggressive than are females.

FERRETS AND CHILDREN
Though children often find ferrets fascinating, carefully consider the age of the children in the household as well as their temperaments before getting a ferret. Some children have a tendency to be rough with animals. While a puppy or rabbit may tolerate this to a large extent, ferrets will nip if they feel threatened and may hang on with their teeth. You should be aware of this and not blame the pet if it happens.

Generally, a child should be eight or older before taking on a ferret as a pet—old enough to understand the ferret's needs and to be responsible in handling it and caring for it. More importantly, adults in the household need to be willing to care for the animal or find it a suitable new home should the child lose interest in the pet.

FERRETS AND OTHER PETS

If you already have other pets, common sense should prevail when deciding whether a ferret can be added to the family. Obviously, you should never let a ferret loose with mice, hamsters, small birds, rabbits or guinea pigs—these are prey species to the ferret. Although the domestic ferret's killing ability is diluted, it may still harm these other animals severely by play-mauling them.

On the other hand, you need to be very protective of your young ferrets if you have dogs and cats. These are natural predators themselves and may badly maul, if not kill, the ferret in their excitement. However, when ferrets and dogs or cats are raised together from a young age, they can become very close companions. Always supervise playtimes in case the dog, in particular, gets over-zealous.

Lively and inquisitive, the ferret makes a fascinating pet for responsible older children and adults.

Bad Reasons to Buy a Ferret

CUTENESS: "It looked so cute and cuddly in the pet shop, we couldn't resist it." Ferrets are cute, but the real issue is whether you are committed to taking care of them for the rest of their lives.

NOVELTY: "We wanted something different from the usual pets." That is fine, but be sure you understand what is involved in keeping a ferret! They require dedicated, rather than casual, attention.

PRESSURE: "Our son/daughter pestered us for one, so we finally gave in." Never purchase any pet for a child unless you are prepared to attend to all of the animal's needs if the child loses interest in it. If you do not want the responsibility, be firm and do not get one.

RECOMMENDATION: "A friend has one and is very pleased with it." You need to consider your own circumstances and your willingness to adapt your lifestyle to this kind of pet.

FREEBIE: "It was given to us for nothing." The initial cost of a pet is small when compared to its lifetime upkeep.

PITY: "We took pity on it—it looked so sad." Never purchase a pet out of pity unless you are prepared to cope with (and pay to resolve) any problems that may come with it.

FASHION: "We were told they are the 'in' pet." It is never a good reason or excuse to obtain an animal as a status symbol or for fashion..

CASH: "We were told we could make some extra cash breeding them." This is totally untrue. Most ferret breeders don't break even with their endeavors.

Crucial Considerations

COST

As with any other pet, there are costs associated with obtaining and caring for a ferret. These include:

- Purchasing a quality ferret from a reliable source.
- Buying the best housing for it you can afford in terms of both size and material construction.
- Providing appropriate food. This is typically inexpensive though special diets are sometimes needed depending on the ferret's health status.
- Ensuring you can afford the necessary vaccinations and future boosters, as well as routine check-ups.
- Ensuring you can afford veterinary care for illness or injury.

If you are not convinced that you can afford to adequately care for a ferret at this time, it would be wise to wait until your finances are more flexible.

LEGALITY

In the past, ferrets were sometimes regulated as wild or exotic pets and some states, such as Hawaii, did not allow them as pets at all. Though this has been changing in recent years, some localities do still restrict or regulate ownership of pet ferrets. Consult your local Department of Agriculture, Department of Fish and Game, town or city hall, or the animal control department to find out what rules are in effect in your area. If you live in a rental property, check and see whether ferrets are among the allowed types of pets. Ferret breeders are also subject to regulations which vary from place to place.

It's also worth noting that if your ferret bites someone and is reported to local authorities, the animal will be quarantined and tested. In some states and counties, the law still requires that the animal be euthanized if rabies vaccination cannot be verified, though this policy is gradually being reversed. The risk of your contracting rabies from a ferret is much less than from a dog, cat, or most other animals, including farm animals. In fact, it is extremely rare for ferrets to get rabies in the first place since they are kept primarily indoors.

Ferrets require a lot of attention and interaction. Do you have the free time needed for handling and training this kind of pet?

COMMITMENT

The ferret is cute, charming, and playful. It is also mischievous and, no matter how mature it gets, will want to "ferret out" new things to carry around, corners to investigate, and places to sleep. Ferrets are also more likely to nip and bite, even when they are just playing, than are most other pets. Can you tolerate this? Can the other members of your household? If the ferret is intended to be a child's pet, are you willing to care for it yourself if the child loses interest?

Most of the time when owners decide to get rid of their ferrets, it's because of the high degree of interaction that the pets require. Although they may sleep 10–15 hours per day, they are very active the rest of the time. They should be allowed out of their cage to play and exercise at least an hour a day, and two to four hours is even better. Do you have this kind of time available? Consider this very carefully before you proceed.

2

SETTING UP:
Getting Ready for Your New Pet

Proper housing should always be purchased BEFORE you buy the ferret. This way you have time to look for a cage that will truly suit your needs, rather than buying something less satisfactory just because nothing else is immediately available. By planning ahead, you can also have all your supplies—food, litter, furnishings, etc.— prepared so that your ferret can settle into his new home with minimal fuss.

The Ferret Cage

When inspecting a cage, ensure there are no sharp internal projections and that the door is big enough for you to reach in and gently take the ferret out. Cages that allow you to open one entire side are ideal because they make it very easy to get the litter box in and out for cleaning. The larger the cage, the better. It should have room for an adult ferret to move around and exercise. Multi-level cages are more costly, but are better than single-level units.

It is recommended that pet ferrets be kept inside the home. This allows maximum interaction between you and the ferret, making your pet more relaxed and affectionate. Historically, when ferrets were kept for rabbit hunting, they were housed

NO AQUARIUMS, PLEASE.
Aquariums are only suitable for small rodents like mice and gerbils. Ferrets require more space and better ventilation than aquariums can provide.

Wire cages like this one are ideal for housing ferrets. Buy the biggest cage that your space and budget will allow.

outdoors in wooden hutches. The main problem with a wooden cage inside the home is that it is almost impossible to keep clean and odor-free. Today, coated wire cages are the best means to house pet ferrets. Wire cages are easy to clean, amply ventilated, and are available in a vast range of sizes, styles and furnishings. Prices depend on quality and features. (Galvanized mesh cages are not recommended.)

DIMENSIONS
The minimum cage size for a ferret is 24 x 24 x 18 inches (62 x 62 x 45 cms) but larger units are even better. Buy the biggest cage your space and budget will allow. Cages can be fitted with casters (small rotating wheels) to make it easy to move them when necessary. Ferrets can escape through surprisingly small holes, so the bars of the cage should be no more than one inch apart (2.5 cms). The bars need to be a half-inch apart or less for young kits. Be sure the housing is sturdy and well-made.

FLOORING
Wire floors are not good for your ferret's feet. If you purchase a cage with a wire floor, see if you can find a rigid plastic floor that will fit inside the cage. Linoleum squares also work.

Commercially-made plastic floor rugs for cages don't last long with ferrets, and can be harmful if pieces are swallowed.

Cage Furnishings

In addition to confining the ferret when you don't want him running around the house, the cage provides a place for three important functions: sleeping, toileting, and playing.

NESTBOX
A ferret needs a cozy place to sleep, so provide it with a small cardboard box or a commercial ferret nestbox. The sleeping box only needs to be about 12 x 9 x 6 inches (31 x 23 x 15 cms) because these pets will curl in a ball when asleep. An entrance hole about 2.5 inches (6 cms) in diameter should be adequate for all but overweight pets. A box this size is actually big enough for two ferrets because they tend to pile on top of each other when sleeping.

There is a whole range of bedding options available for ferrets today. They include hammocks, tents and stylish bedrooms. The key considerations are that the pet has its privacy, and that the furnishings are easy to keep clean. Provide soft bedding like old t-shirts, and wash these frequently since they will absorb the ferret's musky body oils. If you use a cardboard box, exchange it periodically for a new one.

Wood shavings are no longer recommended for small pets. The phenols within the shavings, especially in pine, can create pro-gressive respiratory and other health problems.

LITTER BOX
Ferrets can be litter-trained, although they tend not to be as successful with this as cats are (in other words, "accidents" will happen). Purchase a small plastic litter box and put it in one corner of the cage, as far from the nestbox and food dish as possible—though in a

Place the litter box as far away from food dishes as possible.

19

small cage this does not allow for much distance. Many owners prefer pelleted litter products, such as those made from recycled paper or compressed wood. You can also use a good-quality cat litter that will neutralize fecal and urine odors. "Clumping" cat litters should be avoided since these can irritate ferrets' eyes and respiratory tracts. Clean solid waste out of the litter box every day to minimize odors.

FOOD/WATER CONTAINERS

Ferrets are good at tipping over food and water dishes, so inverted bottle-type water dispensers, and food dishes that clip onto the cage bars, are popular choices. Most ferrets do love to play in a bowl of water, however, so you may want to occasionally put a heavy, earthenware water bowl in the cage, or allow your ferret to play in one when you have him out of the cage. Avoid small plastic containers. If chewed, the swallowed pieces can create intestinal blockages.

Gravity-fed water bottles prevent spills.

TOYS

Ferrets are so playful they will invent games with almost anything available. Try giving them plastic pipes they can run through, cardboard boxes with holes in them, towels, solid (never soft) rubber toys, and rope climbing ladders (ferrets are not expert climbers, but they have fun trying!). They also love things like hammocks they can relax and play in. There are many toys available for these pets, but always inspect them carefully. Cheap toys may contain dangerous wires or small pieces that can be swallowed; or they can be made of plastic which the ferret can tear into pieces.

Finding a Place for the Cage

Housing must be located where the temperature is reasonably constant, never in direct sunlight or exposed to drafts. Don't place the cage in front of exterior doors or close to radiators, air conditioning units, etc.

You can buy all kinds of toys for your ferret, but sometimes the simple ones are best—like this cloth bag or even your old socks.

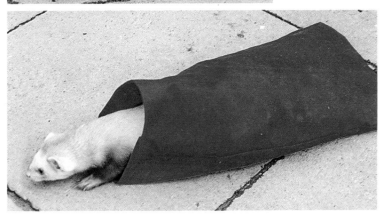

Placing the cage about two or three feet above floor level will make it easier for you to tend to your pet's daily needs, while giving the ferret a better view of what is happening in the room. Ferrets are very social creatures and will do best in a room where you spend a lot of time, rather than in a room that is rarely visited. Ideally, this should be a room that you can "ferret-proof" thoroughly (see below) so that you can often let your pet out of the cage to play and interact with the rest of the family.

Essential Accessories

Here are a few other items you'll want to have on hand:

● A medium-soft bristle brush, comb, and soft cloth for grooming and polishing the fur (see Chapter 4 for grooming tips).

- A pet carrier for transporting the ferret to the vet or elsewhere. Any that are suitable for cats or rabbits will be fine.

- A first-aid kit (see Chapter 6).

- A small harness is useful so the pet can be exercised outdoors. Be sure it is suitable for ferrets. It should fit comfortably but be secure enough that the ferret cannot wriggle out (see Chapter 4 for information about harness training). The harness should be used only when the pet is being exercised, or when visiting the vet or your friends. Collars are not recommended.

You will need a carrier to transport your ferret.

Ferret-Proofing

"Ferret-proofing" means making sure that any room in which the pet will be allowed to roam is carefully checked for dangers and for places these agile animals might escape through or cannot easily be retrieved from. Ferrets are small, quiet, curious, and able to fit into very small spaces—you will have to be very careful when they are out of their cages.

The dangers include trailing electrical wires, cabinets containing potentially harmful contents (paints, chemicals, medicines), indoor plants (which can be poisonous), open fires, aquariums without hoods, power tools left running, irons left on a board, open sewing baskets containing sharp needles, and anything else that an inquisitive ferret might want to pick up, chew on, or explore.

Kitchens are also full of potential dangers: hot burners, pans of boiling liquids/foods, mixers and similar appliances. Do not let them roam freely in the kitchen while cooking and preparation are in progress—you could injure yourself and the pet if it is underfoot when you are carrying hot foods or plates. Make sure cabinet doors are kept closed to discourage exploration.

Ferrets are fragile! When they are on the loose, watch where you step, and especially where you sit (they love to hide under blankets and pillows, etc.) so you don't accidentally injure your pets.

If your ferret finds it easy to open these doors, consider adding child-proof latches. Food pantries must never be left open. A ferret will want to inspect everything, including items it will not actually eat. By nature ferrets are hoarders, so they will transport all sorts of unlikely items to hiding places of their own choosing.

Make sure the windows are closed when the ferret is roaming. A ferret can be hurt if caught in a door that is slamming due to a draft from an open window or from a fan or vent.

If you are painting or working with power tools, confine the ferret so that his curiosity doesn't put him in danger.

You must always be watchful for where the ferret goes and be aware of what it can get into. Any holes in walls or baseboards,

---

FERRET FACTS ON THE INTERNET
The Internet offers an abundance of websites dedicated to ferrets—or "fuzzies," as they are often called by owners. A few Internet searches will lead you to many additional tips on general ferret care as well as ferret-proofing.

even tiny ones, should be sealed. Never leave washing machine or dryer doors open, especially if they contain clothes. To a ferret, this represents a great place to snuggle and have a nap. You could close the door not knowing that it is inside.

The Outdoor Pen

You cannot let a ferret roam freely outdoors or you will soon lose it. In Chapter 4 we'll discuss training ferrets to accept a harness and leash so that you can exercise them outside. As another option, in nice weather you can place the ferret's cage in a shaded spot, or provide it with an outdoor pen. If the pen has a covered area to provide shade and shelter from rain, the pet will enjoy this chance to be outdoors.

For convenience, you may want to purchase a pen for outdoors or build one with a wooden frame and wire mesh fencing. The key factors with outdoor pens are that they must be very secure, with no gaps where your pet could squeeze through, and they must provide shelter from direct sunlight and winds at all times. Ferrets love to bask in the sun but cannot tolerate hot weather. They must be able to retreat to a cooler spot whenever they wish.

Your ferret will benefit from having an outdoor run.

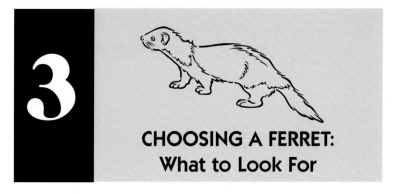

CHOOSING A FERRET:
What to Look For

It's worth doing a little research, and definitely some comparison shopping, before you purchase a ferret. Visit several pet shops and/or breeders to see what types of ferrets are available and how much they cost. Do an Internet search or ask local vets or pet shops to see if there are ferret clubs or shows nearby. Talking with other owners is very helpful in deciding what kind of ferret will suit your needs and where to purchase a healthy ferret. Also, ferrets come in many colors, so it's helpful to see the varieties available before you make your choice.

Look for a ferret that is about 12 weeks of age.

How Much Will the Ferret Cost?

The cost of a ferret depends on numerous factors: age, vaccination status, color, and quality, etc. A typical ferret from a pet shop or reliable breeder will usually cost less than a purebred puppy or kitten, however. Contact several pet shops and/or breeders to get a sense of what the market prices are. Temperament is just as important as color or any other attribute. When you find a charming and inquisitive kit who is a pleasure to handle, it's worth paying a little extra for it.

Age to Purchase

Ferrets are weaned at six to nine weeks of age. It can be risky, however, to purchase a kit who has just been weaned. Its immune system is not fully active yet, and separating it from its mother will be quite stressful. It is better to wait until the kit is 10–12 weeks old and better able to cope with the transition to a new home. The extra weeks make an enormous difference.

Male or Female

Both male ferrets ("hobs") and females ("jills") make fine pets, and there's little reason to prefer one gender more than the other. No matter what gender they are, they are still individuals with their own unique personalities. Concentrate on getting the nicest ferret you can, regardless of its sex.

Colors

The six basic colors of ferrets are described below, but if you are interested in showing or breeding ferrets, you will want to obtain further information about standards from an organization like the American Ferret Association (www.ferret.org).

ALBINO: This is an all-white ferret with pink eyes. It has no visible color pigment. Genetically, it is not devoid of color, but in its double gene dosage, the albino mutation prevents pigments from forming. A very common color.

DARK-EYED WHITE: All white with dark ruby eyes. Not an albino but a separate mutation.

BLACK: Solid black from head to tail, with no discernible pattern.

SABLE: Dark brown body, black feet, and typical polecat mask. A very popular color.

CHOCOLATE: Like a sable, but the legs are brown and the body a slightly lighter color.

CINNAMON: A light reddish-brown, with legs of a somewhat darker shade.

Markings

MASK: This is the way color is imposed on the face in the form of a "T" (full mask) or a "V." There may also be no mask.

MITTS: All four feet are white.

BLAZE: This means white on the forehead and extending down the neck, with a white bib (chest) and mitts on the feet.

Patterns

Pattern refers to the distribution of color on the body. These are the common patterns:

SIAMESE: Also called "color point." The body fur is lighter than that of the legs.

ROAN: This is a mixture of colored and white guard hairs. ("Guard hairs" make up the long, coarse hair that determines the ferret's color).

DALMATIAN: Spots and blotches on a white coat.

SILVER: Dark gray (a mixture of dark and white hairs), some with mitts.

The colors and patterns may be intermixed to create an enormous array of possibilities, such as black roan, chocolate roan, Siamese cinnamon, Siamese mitt, or sable blaze. Some colors and patterns are more readily available than others, depending on the breeders in your area.

If you plan on entering your ferret in shows, you will want to research the standards on colors and patterns before choosing your new pet. On the other hand, there are many ferrets who are "mongrels," not exactly fitting the color/pattern classifications, which will make delightful pets.

One or Two Ferrets?

Ferrets enjoy the company of their own kind and will form strong bonds with each other. Two will provide twice the amusement and companionship of one. When you are not around, they will chase and play with each other just like kittens. For these reasons, two are recommended if you can afford double the cost for caring for them. Don't buy two and end up skimping on booster shots and vet care because you can't afford the increased expense of caring for them properly. It's better in that case to have just one pet who can be very well taken care of.

Ferrets are very playful and enjoy each other's company.

Places to Purchase a Ferret

If you intend to show your new pet, purchasing from a reputable breeder is by far the best option. They will have the colors and quality stock needed for showing. Many breeders maintain Internet sites to promote their business and show their available stock. Some, but not all, are willing to ship animals.

For most people, however, the local pet shop will do just fine. They'll have ferrets to choose from as well as the supplies you'll need for taking care of them. Ferrets are also available for sale or adoption from friends or animal shelters.

It's important to get your ferret from a shop or individual where the animals are well cared for. Are the living conditions clean and well maintained? Are food and water vessels in good condition? If you're purchasing from a pet store, the salesperson should be knowledgeable about ferrets and not try to pressure you into buying. Ask other ferret owners or veterinarians for recommendations about where to buy.

Choosing the Right Ferret

Your first concern should be the health of the animal. If the ferret looks unwell, do not buy it. Consult Chapter 6 for details about signs of illness. A healthy ferret will move around with ease and should not appear lethargic once awake. The pet you

---

SHOULD I BUY AN ADULT FERRET OR A KIT?
The advantage of buying a young ferret is that its history is usually known, while a more mature ferret may have developed bad habits that could be impossible to correct. On the other hand, an adult ferret who has been well trained could more easily be added to your household.

purchase should have received all of the necessary vaccinations, including any boosters.

It is the ferret's temperament, however, that matters the most in your success with it. When you pick up a young kit, it may be hesitant but should relax very quickly and allow you to handle it with ease. If the seller shows reluctance in handling a kit, this may be because the animal tends to bite or be aggressive (although this may just be a sign that the handler is inexperienced with ferrets, as sometimes is the case in pet shops).

Realize too that ferrets have their own distinct personalities. Some kits may be bolder and play-nip at you. Others may nip because they are not in the mood to be handled. They are young and still in the learning stage. However, any signs of obvious aggression indicate a ferret you should avoid.

Ideally, the ferret will be sweet-natured and quick to relax in your arms. This indicates that the animal was reared and handled correctly by the breeder before being offered for sale. Be aware that not all breeders are as attentive as they should be to the importance of early handling and training.

Choose a ferret that is alert and inquisitive and is used to being handled.

CARING FOR YOUR FERRET

Bringing Your Ferret Home

Try to bring your new pet home in the morning. This allows the ferret to settle in during the day while you are around to keep your eye on the process. If you don't have a pet carrier yet, you can bring your ferret home in a sturdy, well-ventilated cardboard box lined with old towels.

Make the return trip home as quick as possible. The ferret should not be exposed to drafts in the car, nor should it ever be left unattended in a car during hot weather. Many pets die every year due to heatstroke from being left in hot vehicles.

Allow your new pet some quiet time to settle into its new environment.

PAPERWORK

Be sure you are given your pet's paperwork. This will include vaccination certificates, pedigree (if applicable), receipt, information about diet, and details of any preventative treatments (e.g. worming) recently performed. Some sellers provide a limited time guarantee—ask for the details before you leave.

ARRIVING HOME

Once home, place the ferret into its housing and allow it to explore, eat, and snooze as it wishes. Let it settle in for a few hours without interruption. Later, you can take your new pet out to explore the room and play a little.

LITTER TRAINING

Initially, the ferret's freedom should be restricted to one room. Be sure this contains a litter box. Do not let the pet into other rooms until you are satisfied that it knows what a litter box is for; then place litter boxes in each room where it has free access. The ferret will usually use the toilet shortly after waking up, after playing, and after meals. At these times you can place it in the litter box until it gets the general idea. Offer treats for using the litter box: positive reinforcement is very helpful!

Be advised, however, that litter training is not always 100% effective with ferrets. This may influence your decision about which rooms the ferret can be allowed to roam in freely. If your ferret continues to use an unacceptable spot for toileting, make sure the spot is thoroughly cleaned to remove the odor and then try placing a dish of ferret food or used bedding there. Ferrets do not want to soil their eating and sleeping areas.

Handling

Your pet must **always** be handled gently but firmly. This fact must be stressed to young children, and strictly enforced if you want the best from your new family member. Ferrets that are handled roughly or thoughtlessly are likely to begin nipping to show their displeasure. Be sure the pet is aware it is about to be handled—don't surprise it by lifting it when it's asleep, half awake, or not watching.

There are two ways a ferret can be lifted. The most common is to place one hand over its shoulders, the fingers encircling its chest.

Picking Up a Ferret

1. *Take a firm hold, one hand encircling the chest, the other restraining the hind legs.*

2. *As the ferret begins to relax, you can loosen your hold on the hind legs.*

3. *Now the ferret is being held with just a light hand on the tail.*

4. *The ferret is completely relaxed and makes no attempt to escape.*

This restricts its movements. It can now be lifted while restraining its hind legs, so that the body can rest on your arm. The second method is to grasp the loose fur at the nape of the neck and then lift the ferret. The ferret will relax because this method mimics the way it was carried by its mother as a baby. You can then support its rear end with your free hand, which makes the hold more secure and more comfortable for the ferret. Always remember that ferrets are fragile animals and it is easy to hurt them. NEVER pull the ferret by its tail.

HOW TO DISCOURAGE NIPPING
Chances are that your ferret isn't trying to hurt you, but they do play rough with each other, which means that they may also play rough with you. Swatting your ferret for nipping you is not recommended. Instead, try these gentler approaches: spray him with a water bottle, blow in his face, or put him in his cage for a "time out."

Feeding Your Ferret

Ferrets are carnivores (meat-eaters) and in the "old days" were fed fresh meat like rabbit carcasses, day-old chicks, and so forth. Obviously, most pet owners today prefer a more convenient way of feeding their pets.

A commercial ferret food will ensure that your ferret's diet includes the nutrients it needs for good health. Some owners use cat food instead and this works well, provided that it is a premium-quality food with protein content of about 32% and fat content of about 20%. Meat should be one of the first two ingredients. Ferrets have little need for carbohydrates, fish, and plant foods. Do not use dog foods or any other kind of pet foods—none of these is suitable for your ferret.

Bear in mind that the drier the food is, the more water the ferret will want to drink. There should be fresh drinking water available at all times.

Ferrets enjoy eating fresh meat or poultry, and you can substitute this for some meals in place of the commercial ferret food. Avoid bacterial contamination that might make your animals sick by giving them only cooked meat, not raw. Cut meat into small slices the pet can cope with easily. Offer beef and similar types of bones, too, since they are good for the ferret's jaws and teeth. Do not give your ferret chicken, rabbit, or fish containing bones; these bones are small and may splinter when bitten or get lodged in the pet's throat or digestive tract.

Ferrets do not need fruits and vegetables in their diet (and some people recommend against feeding them to ferrets), but you can offer small samples of these to see if your ferret enjoys any of them. Milk is unnecessary and too much will cause intestinal problems. Some ferrets enjoy dry, unsweetened cereal, but NEVER feed chocolate as it is toxic for these animals. You should also avoid offering sugary treats of any kind.

Vitamin supplements made specifically for ferrets are available, but do not give these unless so advised by your vet. Some vitamins and minerals are toxic at high doses, so if you're feeding a complete ferret food, the supplement may be too much.

You can supply your ferret with a balanced diet using a good quality ferret food, or cat food with protein content of 30–35% and meat as a main ingredient.

Vitamin and mineral supplements are available for ferrets, but consult your vet before supplementing a complete diet.

Allow your ferret to eat when he is hungry rather than worrying about set mealtimes. Ferrets have a rapid metabolism so they do best with small but frequent meals. If you are feeding dry food, just make sure there is always some food in the bowl.

Ferrets are unlikely to over-eat. Dump out uneaten food at the end of the day because ferrets won't like stale food. If you feed fresh foods, throw away the uneaten portions after the ferret appears to be done with the meal so they don't spoil. It is also important to check for hoarded food in the ferret's cage each day so it can be removed before it rots.

If you decide to change your ferret's main food, doing so gradually is the best approach. Offer a mixture of the old and new food, gradually reducing the proportion of the old food.

Finally, when offering unfamiliar food items, be sure to do so in small quantities in case the ferret is not able to digest them well.

Weight Gain

Pets become overweight for the following reasons: they are not getting enough exercise in relation to food eaten; they are eating out of boredom; they are being fed too many carbohydrates or fats; or they may have a metabolic disorder.

With ferrets, there is usually another reason: during the autumn months these animals naturally gain weight—in the wild, this extra fat layer would provide insulation and food reserves. Some seasonal weight gain is noted with pet ferrets, though it is not as pronounced as it would be in wild ferrets. They will shed this excess weight in the spring.

If your ferret's weight gain seems excessive, consult your vet to rule out a physical condition. Your vet can help you determine whether the problem is metabolic or simply a matter of fine-tuning the pet's diet and increasing its exercise. If you are keeping your ferret caged the majority of the time with few opportunities for exercise, weight gain shouldn't be a surprise!

Grooming and Bathing

COAT
Opinions vary as to how often you should groom a ferret's coat. While some people believe in daily grooming, others find that the occasional brushing is all that's necessary. Not all ferrets enjoy being groomed and this can be an added argument for not doing it too often.

Daily brushing is recommended, however, during the spring and fall when ferrets are shedding.

If you are not comfortable trimming your pet's nails, ask your vet to show you how to do it.

This removes loose hair that your ferret might otherwise ingest while grooming itself and this helps prevent the formation of hairballs. Use a soft bristle brush to gently brush the coat in the same direction the hair grows. Do not apply too much pressure, especially on sensitive parts like the belly and tail, but enough to be thorough. Follow this by combing with a small animal comb to remove any remaining loose hair.

NAILS
Your ferret's nails need to be trimmed every seven to ten days. Untrimmed nails can be painful to the ferret and will snag on bedding, carpet, furniture, etc. You can use manicure clippers or a guillotine-style nail trimmer, but be careful not to cut close to the quick (the pink area) since this will cause pain and bleeding. Keep styptic powder in your first aid kit so it can be used to stop the bleeding if you cut into the quick accidentally. Most owners find that nail trimming requires one person to hold the ferret while a second person does the clipping.

EARS
Once or twice a month, inspect the ears to see if there is waxy build-up. Using a cotton swab moistened with ear-cleaning solution (available from pet stores), clean around the external parts of the ear, following the natural curve. Do not push the

swab into the ear canal. A small amount of mineral oil can be used to soften dried earwax, but you must remove all traces of the mineral oil afterward to prevent it from growing bacteria. You may need a second person to hold the ferret while you clean its ears; this is not a process most ferrets enjoy!

Earwax with a foul odor often indicates that ear mites are present. Likewise, if you see that your ferret is having trouble with balance, or is frequently rubbing its ears against things, earmites may to be blame. Clean the ears with a miticide product from your pet store and see the vet if the problem doesn't clear up in a timely fashion.

TEETH

Inspect your pet's teeth periodically for incorrect alignment, damage, or tartar. Feeding hard foods helps prevent plaque build-up, but weekly tooth-brushing is still important. Use a kitten toothbrush or piece of cloth and pet toothpaste approved for ferrets. Do NOT use human toothbrushes (even soft ones will be too rough for your pet) and do NOT use human toothpaste (it is toxic to ferrets). Additionally, your vet will do a thorough cleaning of the teeth at the ferret's annual check-up.

BATHING

Contrary to what many people expect, frequent bathing does not reduce the body odors of ferrets but actually makes them worse. By removing the natural skin oils, bathing dries out the skin and coat, causing increased production of oils to compensate. You won't notice any difference in the pet's odor, or at least not for long.

Save bathing for when your ferret is very dirty. With regular grooming, your ferret can go for 4–6 months without a bath. When a bath is necessary, use a special ferret shampoo, kitten shampoo, or no-tears baby shampoo. Make sure the bath water is warm but not too hot. Some ferrets are delighted to have a chance to play in the water at bathtime, while others dislike the whole process. Go slowly and speak calmly throughout. Experiment—if bathing the ferret in a dishpan or small tub doesn't work well, try a "shower" instead, rinsing him gently with a sprayer hose. Providing secure footing for him will also help him relax while being bathed. Rinse all traces of shampoo out of his coat and then gently towel him dry.

Bathing

Use lukewarm water in the bath and hold your pet securely. Speak to it calmly.

Use ferret shampoo or kitten shampoo, and rinse thoroughly.

Gently towel your ferret dry.

Some ferrets enjoy bathing (and playing in the water) more than others do.

Odor Control

The ferret's reputation for being odorous has been greatly exaggerated over the years. While its normal body scent is different than that of other pets, many owners find it easy to tolerate.

The key to managing odors is scrupulous attention to cleanliness, particularly of the litter box and bedding. The litter box must be cleaned of solid waste at least once per day and the litter thoroughly changed every few days. If there are plastic toys, hammocks, or tubes in the cage, wash them periodically as well. You can use a very weak solution of bleach mixed in water (about 2% bleach) to clean out the cage, but other household cleaners can be toxic and should not be used.

Bedding should be removed and washed daily, or at least every 2–3 days. Wash bedding items in a detergent free of dyes and perfumes. Having several changes of bedding available makes it easier to swap soiled bedding for clean on a frequent basis. Make sure there is no food hidden in the ferret's cage where it will spoil, and wash food and water dishes each day. Grooming the ferret and bathing it when dirty also helps. In rooms where the ferret is allowed to roam, daily vacuuming is a good idea.

In case of toileting "accidents," clean the spot thoroughly and apply an odor-neutralizing agent (available from your pet shop). Aerosol sprays are useless for removing odors; they

merely mask them for short periods. You may want to cover the spot temporarily so the pet cannot reuse it. If accidents happen repeatedly in the same room, clean the room thoroughly and do not allow the ferret back in there until there is no trace of scent. Odor molecules can penetrate furniture, taking some time to disappear.

If you want to take additional steps to minimize odors, some ferret odor control sprays are on the market. Look for ones that neutralize rather than just cover up odors. Never use air freshener sprays, perfumes or colognes on or near your ferret. Also be careful not to use air freshener solids or plug-ins where your ferret can reach them and possibly try to eat them.

Purchasing an ionizer unit is a more costly approach, but one that can make a big difference, especially if you have more than one ferret in your home.

De-Scenting

The majority of ferrets sold in the United States have already been altered (i.e. spayed or neutered) and de-scented (the anal musk glands have been removed). Since the anal scent glands are only used when the ferret is very frightened, which should occur rarely in pets, removal of these glands doesn't make a significant change in the animal's regular body odor. In fact, neutering has more of an impact on normal body odor than de-scenting does. If you purchase an animal which has not been de-scented, you may want to discuss the pros and cons of de-scenting with your vet or other owners. Opinions greatly vary as to whether de-scenting is necessary or ethical. In many European countries de-scenting is considered an abuse of the animal and is usually illegal. You will have to make your own decision.

Vaccinations

As with any other pet, vaccinations are an important part of keeping your ferret healthy. Regulations on vaccinations vary according to where you live—your vet can give you all the details about what is required and what is recommended. Here is a brief overview of the most common vaccinations:

CANINE DISTEMPER
Vaccination against canine distemper is essential since the disease is fatal to unimmunized ferrets. Young kits receive a series of three shots, at about 8, 11, and 14 weeks of age. Annual booster shots are required.

RABIES

Rabies vaccination is usually required by law, although rabies in ferrets (since they are kept primarily indoors) is extremely rare in the U.S. The first shot is given when the kit is about 12–16 weeks of age, with annual booster shots.

OTHER DISEASES

Opinions vary as to whether ferrets should be vaccinated against illnesses such as feline leukemia and feline distemper. If you have cats in your home, you may want to discuss these vaccinations with your vet.

Spaying and Neutering

Nearly all ferrets sold as pets in the United States are already neutered or spayed when they are offered for sale. Also known as "altering," this is typically done at about four months of age. There are many good reasons for neutering or spaying ferrets, not least of which is the pet owner's responsibility to prevent unwanted offspring.

If spaying is not undertaken, the female's (jill's) life is placed at risk. When the female comes into estrus (heat), she remains in that state until bred. If she does not mate, she can stay in estrus for 4–5 months and can become severely anemic. Bone marrow suppression, vaginal infection, and death are all possible as a result. Should your female ferret come into heat before she is spayed, a hormonal injection at the vet's office can be used to terminate estrus.

In the male's case, neutering will reduce his general body scent and prevent him from getting more aggressive as he matures.

Harness Training

Ferrets are more like cats than dogs where training is concerned. You can teach ferrets to accept a harness and leash, but they won't heel like a dog and will want to go their own way. At best, you can arrive at a compromise where they are allowed to sniff around to satisfy their curiosity, but will go along with you once they feel a few pulls on the leash.

Harness Training

1. With patience and careful handling, you can teach your ferret to accept the harness and leash.

2. Slowly pull the harness over the ferret's head.

3. Fasten the harness behind the front legs.

4. Next, attach the leash.

5. In time, the ferret will enjoy leash-walking as a regular exercise routine.

When leash-training, you must start by letting the ferret become familiar with the feel of its harness (never a collar) while in your home. Be sure the harness is comfortable and fits snugly, but be warned—few harnesses are 100% escape-proof if a ferret becomes very alarmed.

Once the ferret gets used to wearing the harness around the house, begin walking the ferret with the leash attached. Initially, let it go where it wants. Slowly introduce restriction on its movement and encourage it to follow you by calling its name. Reward it when it follows your direction. It may take some days, but eventually it will understand and show some willingness to comply.

Rewards

The ferret can be taught to do a number of things, such as standing on its hind legs or jumping, but the key is to use positive reinforcement and never punishment. When the ferret does what you ask, respond with praise and treats.

Always bear in mind that the best way to train any animal is to focus on the things that come naturally to it. For example, it will be easier to teach a ferret to run through a series of tubes for a reward than it will be to teach it to sit like a dog. Place the ferret at the end of the tube while holding a food treat at the other end. The ferret will soon scurry through for it. Add another tube, and before long the ferret will run through a series of twists and turns just by being placed at one end. Next, give the treat only every second time, and the ferret will still oblige. Eventually, just the occasional treat will be sufficient— the rest of the time the ferret will perform just as well for lots of praise and approval.

FERRET CARE

BREEDING FERRETS

Since most ferrets are already neutered or spayed when they are sold, breeding is not an issue for most pet owners. You may even find it difficult to purchase ferrets for breeding stock, since nearly all on the pet market have already been neutered or spayed. Many breeders will not sell "unaltered" stock unless they are convinced the buyer knows how to properly conduct a breeding operation.

It is best not to consider breeding ferrets unless you are an experienced owner, have a specific objective in mind for your breeding program, and are committed to taking care of and finding good homes for all of the offspring.

If your motive is financial, think again! There is no shortage of ferrets on the market these days. Most breeders invest more money in buying breeding stock and caring for them than they ever get back from selling the offspring. And even a small breeding program entails a lot of hard work for the owner.

If you are committed to starting a breeding program, what follows is a brief overview of the early stages. You will definitely want to do additional reading and research. Talking to established breeders is highly recommended.

Breeding Objectives

Any breeding program should have a specific objective in mind. There is no need to breed ferrets just to produce more ferrets! Here are the three prime goals for hobbyists.

Breeding ferrets should not be taken on by the first-time owner.

TO SPECIALIZE IN THE LESS-ESTABLISHED COLOR PATTERNS:
The idea here is to specialize in a less common color pattern on the chance that its popularity will grow and demand will drive the price up. You will become a breeder associated with the color pattern. Prices for unusual types are always higher than for those readily available—sometimes unreasonable so for short periods. The gamble is that if the color pattern does not gain popularity, you may find it difficult to sell the youngsters.

You may have to search around to find your initial breeding stock, and the animals may be more costly if prices are rising for that particular type. Attending ferret shows before you get started will help you assess the situation regarding various color patterns. Showing your ferrets after you get started with the breeding program will help promote both the color pattern and your business.

TO SPECIALIZE IN QUALITY SHOW STOCK:
In this case you can choose any color pattern, but usually one that is well established. You then attempt to improve the conformation (how well the animal conforms to established physical standards) and color pattern in each successive generation.

You must become a successful exhibitor yourself to achieve your objective. But, ultimately, the value of your stock will increase. This is the most popular objective within the hobby and can be very enjoyable, but it is not as simple as it sounds. First, you must begin with excellent (and thus more costly) breeding stock. Second, competition is fierce—many others are trying to achieve the same objective. Third, it usually takes a while before you are well established as a breeder of quality animals.

TO SPECIALIZE IN QUALITY PET FERRETS:

With this as your objective, you will be especially concerned with temperament—you are trying to breed ferrets which will be affectionate and well-behaved pets. Conformation and color pattern are still going to be important, however. You need to breed for the color patterns that will sell in the greatest numbers. Your initial stock needs to be generally sound in conformation, but outstanding in its temperament. With every generation, this aspect becomes the prime consideration.

Your market will be direct sales to pet owners and shops. While this market may seem to be easy target, it has its problems. There are commercial companies who breed on a large scale for this market and pet stores who rely on them for stock may be unwilling to consider ferrets from smaller breeders. It is also unlikely that you can match the large breeders' prices. You also need to be realistic about how many ferrets you can sell to pet owners in your general area. Research the possible markets—and what it will cost to reach them with advertising and other marketing—before making a big investment.

EDUCATE YOURSELF.
To be a successful breeder, you will need to gain in-depth knowledge of many subjects, including nutrition, general husbandry, record-keeping, health matters, and especially genetics. Reading books about these things will only get you so far—you need to contact people within the hobby who have expertise and are willing to share it. Investigate your target markets and determine how many young ferrets you will realistically be able to sell.

Planning for Breeding

Breeding is a serious business and must be treated as such. You would not open a store without a lot of planning, so apply the same criteria to your breeding operation.

HOUSING
You will require a dedicated breeding room. An outbuilding is usually used for this, such as a garage or shed. It should have electricity, water, and sewage facilities. The breeding room needs to be well ventilated, dry, and equipped with heat and/or air conditioning, as needed in your climate, so that temperature can be regulated at all times. Floors must be easy to clean. Although you will start small, there must be sufficient space to allow for expansion—more cages, more storage, etc.

FITTINGS
Fully-equipped cages are required for each breeding ferret. There must be ample cabinet space and easy-to-clean work surfaces. A small refrigerator for food and medicine is recommended. Outdoor exercise facilities would be very useful. A ferretry can be designed so that each cage or pen has access to its own outdoor run, which does not need to be large, but will be appreciated by the ferrets.

PERMISSIONS
Before you commence preparations for breeding, you must find out if it will be permitted by local ordinances and zoning rules.

Many states require ferret breeders to be licensed and/or inspected—contact your state's Department of Agriculture for further information. You may also need to obtain a license from the United States Department of Agriculture (USDA).

RECORDS

Keep detailed records regarding the health status and breeding of all your animals.

BREEDING STOCK

This can be young and unproven animals (no previous breeding record) or young proven adults. They should be of the highest quality you can afford. Do not begin your breeding program with pet-quality ferrets.

Begin with just a few animals, so if things do not work out as hoped, your commitment is minimal to stock. You can begin with as few as two females (jills) and one male (hob). The females may be of a related or unrelated lineage. The hob should be of the highest standard—he will be mated with numerous jills. This means that his influence on your breeding program will be far greater than that of any single female.

SALES

Attending ferret shows is essential for promoting your business and selling your stock. If you don't live in an area with an active ferret organization and shows, traveling to such shows can be time-consuming and expensive.

HEALTH PROBLEMS

It is always exciting when the babies are born, but can you cope with the problems? Some may be stillborn, deformed, harmed by the mother, or even abandoned by the mother. If the babies become ill, can you afford the vet bills? The jill may also get sick, creating a need for hand-rearing or fostering the offspring.

MONEY AND TIME

As the youngsters grow, so will the bills for food, supplies, vet care, vaccinations, worming, etc. Each baby needs an increasing amount of handling as it nears weaning time. The importance of spending ample time handling the young ones cannot be underestimated if you want buyers to have the same friendly pets that you would want yourself.

Basic Breeding Facts

SEXING: Males are normally larger than females. However, size alone is an unreliable guide. The best way to sex ferrets is to inspect the anal-genital region. The distance between the anus and genitals of the male is longer than in the female. The male's testes are very visible during the breeding period, less so in the winter months.

BREEDING AGE AND STATE: Ferrets become sexually mature at six to eight months old. Breeding from very young individuals is not recommended. Your breeding stock should be at least nine months old and in superb physical condition. The testes

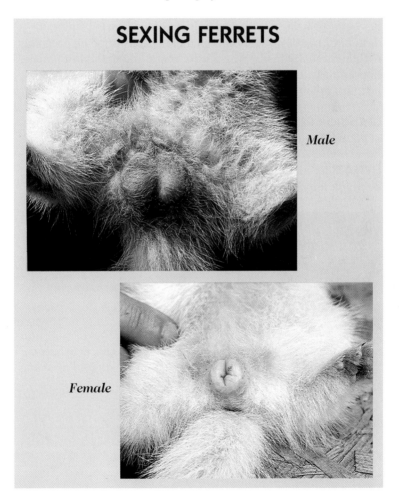

SEXING FERRETS

Male

Female

53

of the male descend into the scrotum during the summer. The vulva of the female starts to swell in the spring and remains in this state until mated. The breeding season is triggered by increasing hours of daylight. The female is an induced ovulator, meaning her eggs are shed by the act of mating, though the male's mere presence may induce this as well.

MATING: It is best to mate a proven hob to an unproven jill, or vice versa. The jill is normally taken to the hob's housing and remains with him until they have mated. If it is clear she is not yet ready to mate, remove her from the cage and try again one to two days later. After mating, return the jill to her own accommodation. Her vulva will start to recede over the next few weeks, the speed of this being governed by how long she has been in heat. She can be palpated for offspring about 30 days after mating. Pseudo-pregnancies (signs of being pregnant without actually being pregnant) are not uncommon in females housed near males or with other pregnant females, and may last just as long as real pregnancies.

GESTATION PERIOD: This is the time between mating and birth of young. In ferrets it is 40–44 days.

LITTER SIZE: An average litter is six to nine kits, but litters can be much larger than this.

The average litter size is between six and nine kits.

At two weeks, the kits will have fur, but their eyes and ears will not open until around three weeks.

By four weeks, the kits will be increasingly active and alert.

Weaning is well under way at six weeks of age.

Kit Development

Ferrets are born blind, deaf, naked and helpless, but develop rapidly. Fur is evident by the end of the first week. Ears and eyes open at 22–35 days. The deciduous teeth (milk teeth) erupt after about ten days, and the canine teeth appear sometime after 45 days. Kits start to crawl within days of birth. By about the ten-day mark, they will be wandering about and being transported back to the nest by the mother.

WEANING: This is finished by six to nine weeks of age, depending on the size of the litter. Once eating independently, the kits should be moved to nursery housing. They can remain together until they are sold or attain sexual maturity.

LITTERS PER YEAR: Two litters per year is the maximum for any female. Some breeders try to produce more than this, but too many pregnancies will compromise both the jill's health and the quality of the offspring.

Non-breeding females can be maintained in their own cages, or in accommodation suitably sized for two or more.

HEALTH CARE

Ferrets, like other pets, can fall victim to a legion of problems and diseases. They can contract illnesses from other pets in the household and even catch colds from the human members of the family. The health of your pet is largely dependent on how you take care of it. With proper nutrition, appropriate preventative treatments, good hygiene and proper handling, the ferret should thrive.

If you think your ferret is ill, do not try to diagnose and treat the problem on your own. Many external symptoms of diseases are very similar and it's easy to misread a major problem as a minor one. Applying an incorrect treatment can worsen the situation. Play it safe and seek veterinary attention—the vet has the training and equipment to make the proper diagnosis and apply appropriate treatment.

Your responsibility is to know your ferret well enough that you will notice, early on, any changes in behavior or condition that might indicate illness. The moment you suspect something is wrong, note the time, date, and what prompted your concern. Observe the animal even more closely from then on. Based on how the problem develops over the next 24 hours, you can decide whether veterinary attention is required.

Signs of Illness

The following are signs that something is wrong. If the problem does not resolve on its own within 24 hours, call your vet.

EXTERNAL SIGNS: Watery eyes, runny nose, swollen nostril(s), misaligned or damaged teeth, bad breath, flaky facial encrustment, excessive or very dark wax in ears, any form of swellings or lumps, abrasions or cuts, loss of hair on any body part, dry lifeless-looking fur, any signs of parasites, blood-streaked fecal matter or urine, evidence of worms around the anus or in the fecal matter, and diarrhea.

BEHAVIORAL SIGNS: Lethargy, inability to balance correctly, limping, vomiting, coughing, sneezing, excessive scratching, lack of interest in food or water, excessive drinking, fur-chewing, pacing, bar-biting, eating fecal matter, excessive sleeping, unwillingness to be handled, pain when handled, excessive panting, wheezing or difficult breathing, straining during urination or defecation, or any other behavior that is not normal for your ferret.

HOW BAD IS IT?
Some of the above symptoms are indicative of nothing more than minor conditions, but it's difficult to be sure. Minor problems usually resolve within 24 hours. Serious ailments do not. Also, the more symptoms displayed by the animal, the more serious the situation.

Take Action

Once you suspect something is wrong with your ferret, you must always make some response. Begin by observing the ferret's condition and behavior more closely. If the symptoms seem minor, the next step is to review the pet's environment. Has the temperature or the pet's diet changed suddenly? Has the pet been in contact with other non-household animals

recently, or are other pets in the family ill? What is the state of the ferret's fecal matter? Could it have eaten some spoiled food or swallowed bits of a toy? Inspect the toys it usually plays with to see if there are missing pieces.

An increase of a few degrees in the general environmental temperature is often very successful in treating minor chills. If the pet is panting and seems lethargic, the problem may be that the temperature is too high. Keeping a thermometer located near the ferret's housing at all times is useful—the temperature near the cage may be quite different from the general temperature on the thermostat elsewhere in the house. Once the temperature exceeds 85°F (29.4°C) your pet may suffer from heat stress.

If the symptoms are more serious, isolate the ferret from any other pets in the household, especially from other ferrets. Then discuss the situation with your vet. Fecal samples should be gathered and placed in a small container to take to the vet.

Common Ailments and Diseases

EXTERNAL PARASITES
These include fleas, lice, and ticks. Regular inspection of the coat by brushing it against its normal direction reveals these unwanted guests. The use of remedies produced for cats or ferrets will normally be effective. Most treatments are topical (on the skin), but injections can be given by your vet. It is

essential when treating parasites that the pet's housing and its general environment be treated also. If any of your other household pets have parasites, your ferret should be treated as well.

INTERNAL PARASITES

The most common of these are worms and flukes of various species. Normally the presence of worms goes undetected, but heavy infestations will become apparent and can cause problems, even death. Do not treat for worms unless the species has been identified. This can only be done by fecal examination and egg counts by your vet, who will supply the appropriate treatment.

WOUNDS

Wounds must be cleansed with lukewarm water to determine the extent of damage. Apply an antiseptic lotion. Minor cuts will heal themselves, but always keep an eye on them in case of secondary infection. More serious wounds require veterinary attention. Wrap the wound with a firm, but not overly tight, bandage to stop the bleeding. Transport the pet to the vet's office as soon as possible. With bad wounds, it may help to wrap the pet in a towel in order to restrict its movements. This will keep it warm and reduce the effects of shock.

HEATSTROKE

Ferrets do not have sweat glands and cannot tolerate temperatures above 85°F (29.4°C). The best prevention, obviously, is maintaining an appropriate indoor temperature and not allowing your ferret outdoors on hot days. Many ferrets die of heatstroke from being left in a hot car, so never leave your ferret unattended in the car. Even a few minutes in an overheated car can kill a small animal.

Signs of heatstroke are heavy panting, mucous discharge from mouth and/or nose, vomiting, swollen lips, staring eyes, and collapse. You must rapidly reduce the ferret's body temperature, especially the head's, otherwise permanent brain damage may ensue. First, place the pet in a shaded, cool location. Next, dip the body in a bowl of cold water, or hold it under a faucet or hose, keeping the head out of the water. Use a wet cloth to stroke the head.

As soon as the pet starts to revive, offer it water to drink. The ferret must be taken to the vet for examination and may need to be treated for fluid loss and shock.

DIARRHEA

This can indicate any number of problems. Mild forms may be caused by a sudden change in diet, eating excessive amounts of bones, or having a cold. These cases usually clear up within 24–48 hours. You can help the situation by reducing or withholding high-protein foods, especially those high in moisture. Should the condition not clear up, and if other signs become apparent, contact your vet immediately. Chronic diarrhea can be life-threatening due to dehydration and loss of vital water electrolytes.

HAIRBALLS

Ferrets are fastidious groomers. In the process, especially in their thicker winter coat, they may swallow enough hairs to cause a partial or total blockage of the digestive tract. When this happens, they soon lose interest in their food and start to vomit. You can prevent or treat hairballs by supplying a ferret laxative or hairball remedy (available in pet stores). In severe cases, veterinary attention is required. Regular grooming, especially during shedding periods, is important for prevention.

BURNS AND SCALDS

A burn is usually noticed immediately because the fur is singed or burnt away. Scalds are caused by chemicals or hot liquids

and may go unnoticed for longer periods. Both are painful, and thus difficult to treat. The first step is to clear the surrounding area of any dirt, using soap and water. Next, with a burn, any loose or burnt skin should be gently wiped away with a very mild saline solution before applying a sterile dressing and bandage.

Scalds will leave the hairs intact and these must be carefully clipped away, if possible, before cleaning and bandaging the affected area. Chemical scalds need to be neutralized if the chemical is known. Use vinegar and water on alkaline burns, bicarbonate of soda on acidic burns. Unless very minor, all burns and scalds should be inspected by your vet at the earliest opportunity.

DISEASES
Ferrets are susceptible to a variety of diseases, some of which are quite serious. Here are a few of the more common ones:

Adrenal tumors develop in many ferrets at around three years of age. The cause is unknown, but the most obvious sign is hair loss and red flaky skin, especially around the tail and back. Females may also have swelling of the vulva, and males with this disease may become more aggressive. Surgery is usually the best option.

Insulinoma, also known as pancreatic beta cell tumor, mainly affects older ferrets (ages 4 and up). The primary symptom is extreme lethargy due to low blood sugar. There are medical and surgical treatments that may be used depending on the age and condition of the ferret.

Lymphoma is a deadly cancer that can affect ferrets of any age. Ferrets will be lethargic and may lose a significant amount of weight. Enlarged lymph nodes are also present. Chemotherapy may be an option depending on how advanced the disease is.

Cardiomyopathy is the enlargement and weakening of the heart muscle. This is difficult to diagnose because the symptoms are so subtle. The animal may be lethargic and have some difficulty breathing or coughing. Medical treatments can slow the progression of the damage.

First-Aid Kit

A well-stocked first-aid kit is essential so that you can quickly respond to accidents and health issues. You can purchase various-sized kits from your vet or pet shop, or make up your own. Ensure that the first aid kit is kept out of reach of curious children and pets.

EMERGENCY ITEMS:
- towels (paper and cloth), cotton swabs, cotton balls, gauze pads
- eye ointment/liquid, antibacterial ointment
- antiseptic cream/powder/liquid, styptic powder/pencil/liquid
- bicarbonate of soda, vinegar, rubbing alcohol, hydrogen peroxide
- scissors (straight and curved blunt-ended)
- tweezers (pointed and blunt-ended)
- magnifying glass, fine-toothed comb, rectal thermometer
- eye dropper, tongue depressors (also useful as splints)
- nail-trimmer, 1 cc syringe, small flashlight or pen-light
- self-adhesive elastic bandages of various sizes
- a few ice packs in your freezer

MEDICATIONS:
Consult your vet to see which medications you should keep on hand, such as antibiotics, laxatives, treatments for diarrhea and upset stomachs, cold treatments, and electrolytes in case of dehydration. Be sure all medicines are stored in cool, dry cabinets or refrigerators and are out of reach of ferrets and children.

Antibiotics have a limited shelf life: discard them after their stated expiration date. Never use antibiotics unless under the direction of a vet. Overuse or misuse has resulted in many drugs becoming ineffective due to bacteria developing resistance to them.